REAL ESTATE AGENTS DON'T SELL HOMES

This is an IndieMosh book

brought to you by MoshPit Publishing
an imprint of Mosher's Business Support Pty Ltd

PO Box 147
Hazelbrook NSW 2779

indiemosh.com.au

First published 2016 © David Kaity

The moral right of the author has been asserted.

All rights reserved. No part of this book may be reproduced or transmitted by any person or entity, in any form or by any means, electronic or mechanical, including photocopying, recording, scanning or by any information storage and retrieval system, without prior permission in writing from the author and publisher.

Cataloguing-in-Publication entry is available from the National Library of Australia: http://catalogue.nla.gov.au/

Title:	Real Estate Agents Don't Sell Homes: What no real estate agent will ever tell you, but all home owners must know before selling
Author:	Kaity, David
ISBNs:	978-1-925447-89-7 (paperback edition)
	978-1-925447-90-3 (ebook – epub)
	978-1-925447-91-0 (ebook – mobi)

Cover design and layout by Ally Mosher at allymosher.com

REAL ESTATE AGENTS DON'T SELL HOMES

What no real estate agent will ever tell you, but all home owners must know before selling

DAVID KAITY

Disclaimer:

The information in this book is general in nature and does not take into account the reader's personal circumstances. Readers should consider whether the information contained in this book is appropriate to their needs, and where appropriate, seek professional marketing advice. The author or his representatives will not be held responsible for the actions or inactions of any individual based on the information contained in this book. Any critique of the real estate sales industry or real estate agents in general is based on personal experience and are not intended to be, nor shall they be, construed as slander or defamation.

Contents

Disclaimer: v

What you will learn from this book 1

Introduction 3
   My personal story 3
   Why are real estate agents generally disliked? 5

Five reasons people choose to use real estate agents 10
   Sir Richard Branson 12
   The alternative to the traditional method of selling 13

Myth 1: Real estate agents sell properties 16
   Why do real estate agents claim that they sell properties? 19
   What do real estate agents really sell? 20

Myth 2: Real estate agents do all the work and make the process easy and convenient 29

Myth 3: "I have a database of buyers ready to buy" 33

Myth 4: "Open homes are the best way to display your home" 38
   Inspections by appointment 46

Myth 5: "I am an expert negotiator, trained to get you a higher price" 54

Myth 6: The local area expert 65

Myth 7: The frenzy of an auction achieves a higher price 70

The better way to sell – trust the process, not an agent ... 76
    Presentation 78
    Pricing 80
    Promotion 82
    Marketing as an investment 84
    A better way to sell 87

What you will learn from this book

- The five wrong reasons why most Australians use a real estate agent and why you should avoid them.
- Why interviewing 3, 10 or 15 real estate agents won't make a difference to the success of selling your home.
- What real estate agents **really** sell.
- The number that is far more important than the price you sell for and why no agent talks about this.
- Why knowing the value of your home has little to do with getting the highest price.
- Why it is deceptive to think that agents make the process of selling convenient.
- The **real** truth behind the 'database of buyers' real estate agents claim to have.
- Why having an open home is often the worst possible way to display your property.
- Why commissions remove any incentive for an agent to get you the highest sale price.

- Why being the 'local area expert' doesn't mean that an agent will perform well or achieve the highest price.
- Why auctions are often better for the buyer and the agent than for the vendor.
- The actual recipe behind any successful property sale and why you need to trust the process instead of a real estate agent.
- The huge benefit of considering marketing as an investment instead of an expense and where you should spend your marketing budget for maximum return.
- The best way to sell any home successfully.

Introduction

My personal story

How does a person come to write a book with such a bold title? What qualifies and inspires someone to devote an entire book to contradicting something that generations have taken for granted? The answer is complicated by the fact that I seem like an unlikely candidate for this task. I spent the first 12 years of my career in the finance industry, with my last role being the senior credit analyst for the finance arm of a well-known industrial manufacturing multi-national.

My true skills lie in being able to see the underlying dynamics behind issues that most people take for granted. At the risk of blowing my own trumpet, I'm also pretty good at tapping into human emotions and the things that make people tick. My passion lies in wheeling and dealing in the property market and the synergy of these skills and passion has resulted in the amazing experiences that I've had, which lead me to write this book.

My knowledge of the workings of the Australian real estate sales industry stems from several years of investing actively in the property market, whether through renovating and holding, renovating and selling, or flipping development sites. Like most budding investors, my wife Zsofi and I made our share of mistakes early in the game and one of these was to overcapitalise on our very first renovation project.

When it came time to sell this property, we would have made a loss if we had to pay commission to a real estate agent. By this stage, we had a very good understanding of what agents did and didn't do, should and shouldn't do, so we decided to attempt to sell privately. We went on a steep learning curve in the process, but in the end we sold successfully, saved approximately $20,000 by not paying a commission or marketing fees and, as a result, broke even on that project.

After having sold our first renovation project privately, we made it our mission to find out everything we could about the real estate sales industry and why it is so disliked by many Australians. During this process, we had the privilege of meeting many remarkable people who had left the industry. They spilled the beans to us on its internal workings and what goes on behind the scenes, where most Australians never get to look.

What we found out was incredible and we came to

understand why the industry is broken and why it all too often lets down the very people it is meant to serve. Unfortunately, operating within this broken system, even the very best people can achieve only mediocre results, because they are hamstrung by the limitations that are set on them by their agency, their principal, their franchise, and the industry itself, which hasn't fundamentally changed the way it operates for several decades.

Operating within this broken system, even the very best people can achieve only mediocre results.

Why are real estate agents generally disliked?

Over the years that we have been transacting property deals, we have met or dealt with well over one hundred real estate agents and amongst them were some very fine upstanding men and women who were professional, friendly, knowledgeable, helpful and generally very good at what they do.

You would be lucky to have some of them as your friends. Like most of us, they are daughters and sons, mums and dads with children and mortgages. We often felt sorry for these people, because as real estate agents they usually get a very bad rap from the general public.

There is an annual poll conducted by Roy Morgan, which looks at the perceived ethics and honesty of various professions. Real estate agents consistently rank in the third lowest position, just above advertising people and car salesmen. I think this is unfair to many real estate agents, but I also know why they generally have such a bad reputation. Of course it doesn't help that they charge such a horrendous sum of money for what they do – and rest assured that their commissions are completely unjustified – but this is not the biggest reason for their bad reputation.

The two main reasons for their poor reputation are the legislation that oversees their operation and the fact that the industry itself is broken and unwilling to change with the times. People looking to engage a licensed real estate agent may feel assured by their qualification and registration under the relevant Act in their respective state.

What many people don't know is just how low the bar is set to enter this profession. For example, in Queensland, for about $600, almost anybody can become a licensed and practicing real estate agent within a few days of undertaking a very easy course. People place their trust in the government bodies that regulate this industry. However, these bodies are letting vendors down by setting very low standards and having weak systems of governance.

In an article in the *Daily Telegraph* on 1 December 2015, Kathryn Welling quoted the president of the Real Estate Institute of NSW, John Cunningham: "You have to do more training to become a barista than you do a real estate agent". He went further and said "There are stories of agents being trained in a matter of hours online". You would never trust the wonderful people making your delicious morning coffee to sell your million-dollar house, yet there are many real estate agents out there with even less training willing to take around $30,000 in commission to do just that.

To be fair to real estate agents, the training required to be able to help someone sell their home successfully does not require years, but neither does this knowledge and work justify the levels of commissions that are charged by the industry. The reasons why real estate agents can get away with charging what they do is detailed in the next section.

Of course the potential for very lucrative commissions attracts all sorts of players, many of whom have questionable motives and integrity, and because this is one of the easiest and cheapest professions to enter in Australia, you generally see the numbers of real estate agents explode in boom times and collapse in slow times.

When I said earlier that the industry is broken, what I meant was that there is a misalignment between the interests of the vendors and the interests of the agents. In effect, what is good for the vendor is not always good for the agent and vice versa. Success for the agent does not necessarily mean success for the vendor, which is why it can be very dangerous to engage a seemingly successful real estate agent.

> *What is good for the vendor is not always good for the agent and vice versa.*

Unfortunately, this is exactly how most Australians choose the agent they will list with. The traditional real estate sales industry operates in a way that does not truly incentivise agents to act in the best interests of property vendors and there are many examples of this given later in the book.

Notes

Five reasons people choose to use real estate agents

1. **They think that there is no other viable alternative.** Some people even think that they are legally required to use a real estate agent to sell their property, while others think that choosing between three or four agents is having choice enough. What they don't realise is that in reality, these three or four agents from different agencies will be working in the same system, playing by the same rules, and using similar tactics, even if they have slightly different approaches. In addition, they will all charge you a commission and most likely, a hefty marketing fee.

2. **People forget.** Even if people have had a previously unpleasant experience, they will sell with a real estate agent again, because this is the kind of transaction that most people only engage in once every seven to ten years on average. Generally, this is enough time for most people to forget the experience, even if it was unpleasant.

3. **The large cost of using agents is disguised.** The cost – however horrendous – comes out of the equity in the property, so it doesn't hurt so much. People are not handing over thick wads of hundred dollar bills or clicking on the 'transfer' button to pay the agent $15,000, $20,000 or $30,000. People never see the money they pay to their agent and so they don't feel the pain of paying it.

4. **Lack of knowledge about what really sells a property.** Most vendors don't understand what makes people buy property, or put another way, they don't understand what factors contribute to the successful sale of a property. This is ironic considering that most people, who are selling, will have bought at some stage, and if they reflected on the circumstances of their purchase, they would gain some valuable insights into what made them buy in the first place.

Most people who really think about what made them buy their home will admit that the agent had very little to do with not just their buying decision, but much of the rest of the process.

If vendors really appreciated the recipe, or the process that lead to a successful sale, they would look for other alternatives to the very expensive traditional real estate agents. Agents know this and so they play their cards very close to their chests, revealing little about this recipe or the components to a successful sale. They know that if they don't hoard this information, they will quickly become irrelevant.

5. **Conditioning by the industry.** There are a number of myths that people have been conditioned to believe about this industry. These myths have become deeply entrenched in the Australian psyche over several decades, thanks mainly to conditioning by the real estate sales industry.

You will not hear the following information from any real estate agent now working in the industry. They will strongly deny everything you are about to read in this book. The following pages uncover these myths and reveal the real truth behind the doctrines of this industry, which most Australians now take for granted. **I will explain why the real estate sales industry is broken and why it is time for a change.**

Sir Richard Branson

On his visit to Australia in 2015, Richard Branson identified the Australian real estate sales industry as one that is ripe for the kind of disruption that is being brought about by the likes of Uber and Air BnB in their respective industries. This is often labelled as digital disruption, when in fact it's much more profound than that. Indeed, technology makes this kind of disruption possible, but the end result and the real change is the vendor-to-customer or peer-to-peer contact and interaction it creates.

Uber puts owner/drivers of vehicles directly in touch with commuters, while Air BnB connects owners of real estate with travellers seeking accommodation. The common factor is the lack of a traditional intermediary or middle-man and instead, we are seeing a return to how business was done a long time ago – person to person, face to face. The human element of doing business is making a resurgence, and people who don't realise this and take advantage of it will be left behind.

The alternative to the traditional method of selling

After I outline the myths, I will also shed light on a new and significantly better alternative to the traditional method of selling that is providing just this type of disruption. This method helps people to achieve the highest possible price for their property at a much lower cost. As a result, most people walk away with, somewhere between $10,000 to $50,000 more – in some cases much more – from the sale of their property, than they would with the traditional way of selling.

Most people walk away with somewhere between $10,000 to $50,000 more.

Notes

Myth 1:
Real estate agents sell properties

Think back to when you bought your home. What made you buy it? If you were dealing with a real estate agent, did they actually do or say anything to sell you the property? Like most buyers, you probably saw the property advertised on the internet; you had a look at the pictures and thought they were interesting enough to justify a closer look.

You probably went to the open home, looked around and within about ten minutes decided that you liked what you saw. You probably made an offer to purchase and maybe it was accepted. Otherwise, there may have been a couple of counter offers, but in the end you signed the contract and bought the property.

It is likely that even before you set foot in the property you knew what your budget was, how many bedrooms and bathrooms it needed to have, what general condition it had to be in, how large the living areas or the block of land needed to be, and what general area it had to be located in. When you inspected a property and it did not fit your criteria, was the agent able to say or do anything to make you change your mind?

Were they able to sell you a property that you did not want to buy? Were they able to convince you to buy something you didn't like, especially when so much money was at stake?

Of course not. You went there with certain expectations and certain criteria, and if the property met them, then you made an offer to purchase. You did not need to be sold on the property.

There is a big difference between you buying a property and an agent selling it to you.

There is a big difference between you buying a property and an agent selling it to you, but very few people are consciously aware of this difference. Following this logic, if you bought the property you are living in and it wasn't sold to you by a real estate agent, why would you think that you should pay a commission to an agent to sell the property to someone else?

So if real estate agents don't sell properties, what does? The answer is surprisingly simple, yet most Australians don't know it. There is a process or a recipe to selling any property successfully and this process doesn't care who follows it. Real estate agents are certainly not the only people who know this recipe and you definitely don't have to pay a huge commission to have this recipe working for you. It consists of a relatively simple three step process called the three P's – Presentation, Pricing and Promotion, around which a campaign is built and which I will explain further in this book.

Nobody can sell a house.

The single biggest contributor to the success of any property sale is the strength of the marketing campaign, which is not to be confused with advertising. Nobody can sell a house. The best you can do is to execute a strong, strategic marketing campaign that results in targeting and attracting the right buyer who is enticed and feels compelled to pay top dollar. Real estate agents are not trained in marketing, but only advertising. When they speak about marketing packages, they are really talking about advertising packages. Advertising is one of the last steps in the marketing process, which alone is not enough to produce a great result.

Why do real estate agents claim that they sell properties?

If real estate agents don't sell properties, then why would most of them make this claim? Why would they not simply say that they are following a strategy, process or recipe?

From my experience, there are three reasons for this. Firstly, many of them have very large egos. This makes it hard for them to admit that they are simply following and implementing a process or a recipe, which is really what sells any property. A large ego needs to take the credit for the success that resulted from following a process. It simply wouldn't make sense for a real estate agent to reinvent the wheel each time they list a property to sell. Instead, they follow the same recipe with small variations depending on the home they are marketing. It is not the person or the personality that sells the home, because buyers are only interested in the property, which is about to become the biggest purchase of their lives.

The second reason most agents claim to sell properties is because they genuinely believe this to be true. They don't understand that the process or recipe is actually what results in the successful sale of a home. They simply don't understand the principles of marketing and why people buy. This second reason is worse than the first, because it signals incompetence on part of the agent. Becoming a real estate agent requires very little training, experience, knowledge, time and cost. The low barriers to entry into this profession mean that the standards are also very low and this often comes at the expense of competence.

The third and final reason why real estate agents may claim to be the ones who sell properties is simply dishonesty. This requires very little explanation in itself. There are agents out there who are experienced and have been around long enough to know that there is a process behind the successful sale of any home, they just simply won't say so. I have lots of respect for those real estate agents who are humble, wise and competent enough to acknowledge that they are expert executioners of a proven process.

What do real estate agents really sell?

Let's not forget though that real estate agents are sales people, but if they don't sell properties, then what do they sell? The answer is very simple. They sell mainly two things. Firstly, they sell themselves to get the listings and secondly, they sell expensive and often unnecessary marketing packages and processes, including auctions.

Real Estate Agents Don't Sell Homes

One of the ways in which many agents sell themselves is to give you a high initial valuation for your property, in the hope that an impressive price will entice you to list with them. When home owners interview two or three agents who may propose similar strategies, tactics and approaches, but one of them offers to a sell for a higher dollar value, there is a good chance that they will choose that particular agent. It may be that that the quoted price is unrealistic and impossible to achieve. However, it has accomplished its goal of a signed contract with the agent.

This will buy the real estate agent time to implement the second part of this strategy, which is to start conditioning you down to a more realistic price. They do this by saying things like "The market has changed" and "The feedback indicates that the price should be lower". This is why it is a big mistake to choose a real estate agent based on the expected sale price they try to win your business with. Some people are aware of this strategy and several former real estate agents have confirmed this for me. One of them said that this strategy is taught and encouraged at one of Australia's largest and best known franchised agencies.

The reality is that neither real estate agents nor valuers can put an exact value on a property. As a good example of this, my wife and I bought a house a couple of years ago, for which the vendor commissioned a valuation from one of

Australia's most reputable registered valuers. The vendor insisted that if we wanted to purchase the property we would have to pay the figure stated on the valuation.

Neither real estate agents nor valuers can put an exact value on a property.

We were happy to oblige and then proceeded to sell the same house a month later for 40% more than what we paid for it. To our benefit, not only did we know the market better than the vendor, but also better than the valuer. The discrepancy between the two 'values' surprised even us. Although valuers are usually far more reliable in their accuracy, due to a lack of a vested interest, the actual selling price will only be determined by the vendor and the buyer on the date when the property changes hands.

Property owners looking to sell should look to narrow down the value of their home to within a $10,000 – $30,000 range, depending on the value of their property. This range is more realistic, much easier to determine and it will be the range within which most realistic offers will be received.

It is enough to know this range in order to achieve the

maximum sale price for a property, because the key is how this price range is communicated to the target audience. Not only is it almost impossible to pin down an exact value for a property, contrary to popular belief you simply don't need to know the exact value to attain the highest possible price for it when selling.

You don't need to know the exact value to attain the highest possible price for it when selling.

The other method real estate agents use to sell themselves to get your listing is to show you very impressive and expensive glossy magazines in which other properties have been showcased. It can be enticing to think that your property could appear in the same glossy magazine as those multi-million dollar homes on the cover pages. These expensive magazines have a similarly low success rate of finding a buyer as having your property displayed in the window of the agency. **These are not the places where people look for a home to purchase any more.**

These glossy magazines are not designed to sell your

property, they are designed to impress you to list with the agent or agency that gave them to you. The money to print these flashy magazines comes from the expensive marketing packages that agents sell to you. Have you noticed that many 'For Sale' signs used by real estate agents at the front of houses for sale often advertise the agency or the face of the agent? This is a classic example of the agent using your advertising budget to advertise themselves or the agency, instead of showing pictures – at least one – of the inside of your home.

On a recent drive through a neighbouring suburb, I noticed a large billboard with two photos of an obviously up-market home. Driving at 60 kilometres per hour, the only information that I picked up was the name of the real estate agent. Being particularly sensitive to this type of advertising from agents, I made an effort to make out the address of the property, but couldn't. I shuddered at the thought of the amount of money that was cajoled out of the vendor by this particular agent under the guise of 'advertising'. It was definitely effective advertising. However, it wasn't targeting the market the vendor was trying to reach, because people don't buy homes from billboards. It was aimed squarely at owners of other luxury properties who are looking for an agent to list with.

Unfortunately, many owners of luxury homes fall for the

trap of thinking that a 'prestigious' agent or agency, or one specialising in high end homes is the best one to market their home. These agents have simply developed an image to appeal to this niche, where the commissions are higher. They have also developed the skills to push the specific 'buttons' of these home owners by appealing to their status and specific emotions.

The unfortunate vendor, who was convinced to pay for the billboard to advertise their luxury property was a typical victim of this practice. The value of a prestige agent falls into the same category as the 'local area expert', which I cover under Myth 6.

At a recent networking function held at the Brisbane offices of Newscorp Australia, an employee was giving my wife and I a brief tour of the building where some of the major local newspapers are created. I was surprised to hear from this employee that about a quarter of the income from their publications is generated by real estate advertisements from real estate agents using the vendors' precious funds. Despite the fact that the vast majority of Australian home buyers search for their next property online, most agents still insist on wasting vast amounts of their vendors' marketing dollars on the increasingly irrelevant and dying print media.

Many real estate agents also try to convince you to 'upgrade' to a premium online advertising package, costing many thousands of dollars, to have your property displaying before others in a search result for a given suburb. By doing this, the agent and the agency also gain prominence at the top of the page, using your marketing budget. These 'premium' ads allocate more space to the face and logo of the real estate agent, at your expense.

In many suburbs, there may only be a small number of properties for sale of a given category (price, number of bedrooms, etc.), which means that people who are searching online for real estate listings under that given category don't have to scroll very far to see what is on offer. Paying for a premium advertisement in these cases is a complete waste of money, but many agents will still encourage you to spend it.

In addition, when people search by map on real estate listing sites for properties in certain streets or suburbs, all properties in those areas will be shown simultaneously, regardless of whether they are expensive premium ads or much cheaper standard ads. Despite this, many real estate agents make it a priority to extract as much money as possible from you for marketing.

A former agent told me how proud one of his colleagues was when he convinced a vendor to hand over $6,000 in marketing fees alone, when he already knew someone who was very interested in buying the property, without the need for any advertising. In this case, not only did the vendor part with a large sum of money for commission, but he also paid an unnecessary marketing fee. This same agent told me that many of his colleagues made a sport of how much they could convince people to spend on marketing, regardless of whether it was necessary or not.

Notes

Myth 2:
Real estate agents do all the work and make the process easy and convenient

Selling a home that you live in is not very convenient.

Unfortunately, this is another common myth that most vendors fall victim to. The simple fact is that selling a home that you live in is not very convenient. No real estate agent can ever make the process completely convenient and eliminate the work that you still have to do. If an agent tells you otherwise, they are dishonest, and if this is the reason you choose to sell with one, you are deluding yourself. Whether you sell with an agent or not, you will still need to become involved in the process and do quite a bit of work, like it or not.

A good real estate agent may point out what preparations need to be undertaken before your house can be advertised and they may even suggest the right contractors for the job. However, you need to organise these yourself. This could mean coordinating with a painter, or doing it yourself, doing the gardening, or calling a handyman to carry out any repairs.

You will also have to de-clutter and keep the home clean for the entire campaign. If the home is to be styled, you need to ensure that it looks like that before every open home or inspection, which means, for example, making all the beds, getting rid of all the shoes from the entrance and removing any pet bowls that may be lying around. No real estate agent will do any of these things for you.

There is an inconvenience in preparing for the open home as well, with the effort that goes into tidying up and creating the feeling of a display home as much as possible. You need to leave the home for 40 minutes and maybe even an hour, and this is certainly not a convenient thing for anybody. When it comes to potential buyers, you will still have to deal with them and their questions, except you will have to do it through your real estate agent.

The agent won't know the answers to many of the specific questions relating to your property, so expect phone calls to clarify many of these with you. Similarly, if there are negotiations, you will still have to be involved, except you will have to negotiate through your real estate agent. You may even wonder whether the agent is on your side or the buyer's during this process.

Just when you thought that your involvement in the process is over, the paperwork starts. This not only means signing the contract, but potentially initialling it a couple of times, if counter offers are made on the contract instead of via verbal negotiations. Even after the contract becomes legally binding, your solicitor or conveyancer will ensure that you have even more paperwork to complete and sign before settlement can take place.

No real estate agent will ever completely eliminate or assume all the work, time and effort that you will have to put into these tasks. For these reasons, using a real estate agent in the belief that he or she will make the process convenient is one of the greatest misconceptions, and a very expensive one at that.

Notes

Myth 3:
"I have a database of buyers ready to buy"

The above claim is used by most real estate agents to try to entice you to list with them. This statement sounds impressive because it implies that the agent personally knows a number of qualified buyers who are ready to purchase your property at a moment's notice. Unfortunately, most people are never told the reality behind this 'database of buyers' claim.

If you were a serious buyer, would you be satisfied with being on the database of one real estate agent and patiently waiting for that agent to suggest potential properties for you to look at? I suspect you are likely to do what most serious buyers do, and that is search the online listings of popular real estate websites. You would also go to several inspections and talk with as many agents about what you are looking for. Why would anybody think that any agent would have an exclusive database of patient buyers, who are not on the database of other agents?

When somebody goes to an open home or an inspection by appointment, the agent will take their name and number and often their email address. Many people, especially at an open home, are not serious buyers and some of them will simply be neighbours, people from down the road or general 'sticky beaks'. By registering their details at the open home – which they are legally required to do – they will go on the agent's database, however, the value of many of these people as potential buyers is questionable.

Even if most people on an agent's database were serious qualified buyers, they will inspect a number of properties during their weekends of searching and will also go on to the database of several other agents. In addition, they will also be looking for properties on the internet. After these people finally purchase a property, do you think they will contact all the agents whose databases they are on to let them know that they are no longer in the market?

In short, most people on these so called databases are either not serious buyers, are likely to have purchased already, or will be on the databases of several other agents. No agent can claim to have an up to date, truly unique and exclusive database of buyers who are waiting solely for that agent to show them potential properties to buy.

Even if a real estate agent claims to know of one or two

qualified and serious buyers, wouldn't you want your property to have greater exposure to a wider market than just a couple of people whom that agent claims to know? It can sound tempting when a real estate agent talks of a potential serious buyer who is ready to purchase, but that person may not be willing to pay what your property is worth because they don't have to compete against many other potential buyers.

Have you ever wondered, that if having a database of buyers is truly a key benefit of using a real estate agent, then why do most of them try to sell you unnecessarily expensive advertising packages? If they have all the right buyers lined up, you shouldn't need to spend any money on marketing, should you?

No agent can claim to have an up to date, truly unique and exclusive database of buyers.

When selling, there is no substitute for giving your property maximum exposure and visibility to as wide a market as possible, by advertising on the most popular real estate listing websites relevant to your area. This is also the best way to create competition for your property, which can help to achieve a higher price.

Fortunately, you no longer have to engage a real estate agent or pay a commission to harness the reach of the internet. Tapping into the bigger market is far more valuable than any real estate agent's claimed database, especially considering how that database is created and the quality of its content.

Notes

Myth 4:
"Open homes are the best way to display your home"

Most people automatically associate selling a property with open homes and they wouldn't even think that there could possibly be another better way of displaying their property for sale to potential buyers. The reality is that open homes are not the best way to display a property for sale, but traditional real estate agents will never tell you this, because this is their preferred method for a number of reasons.

Traditionally, open homes were the best place for agents to prospect for their next customer and this is still the case. For many people, in order to buy a home, they also need to sell one and agents are in a great position to find this out when they are welcoming people to an open home. "Do you need to sell?" is a standard question they ask people who attend and it is one of the reasons why they send you away from your home while the open is held.

Agents don't want you to see that they are using your open

home as an opportunity to look for their next customer, instead of focusing on highlighting the positive attributes of your home to potential buyers. Another reason why real estate agents send you away while the open home is being held is because they don't want you to see how easy the process is. This is exactly why many busier real estate agents and larger agencies will send their juniors to conduct the open.

There is nothing an agent can do there to make people buy.

Real estate agents also prefer open homes because it is one of the few times that they will have the opportunity to be seen to be putting 'effort' into the campaign. I deliberately used inverted commas for the word effort, because there is not much work to be done at the open home, and there is nothing an agent can do there to make people buy. Despite this, they need you to see the 'effort' they are making by turning up at every open in order to justify the unjustifiable commission that they will charge you.

Think back to the open house where you first saw the home you are living in. What impact did the agent have on your buying decision? Were you influenced by the way the agent conducted the event or what they said about the home? Did you buy it because the agent was well dressed, drove a nice car and had nice marketing brochures? If you were like most serious buyers, I suspect that the reasons you bought the home were because you liked its location, condition, presentation, size and number of rooms, not to mention that it was probably within your budget.

I would even suggest that you would not have cared much about who showed you the property, because you were perfectly capable of having a look around to decide whether it was what you were looking for.

The simple truth is that serious buyers go to open homes because of the home and not because of who is presenting it. Many people incorrectly believe that a well-dressed agent with an expensive car, flashy office, glossy brochures and signs with their face on it are what sells the property.

These things are definitely designed to sell, but all they sell are the agent and the agency to prospective vendors who fall for this display. The sole purpose of these tools is to impress you and entice you to list with that agent when it comes time to sell your home. If these superficial and showy displays did not play a part in your last buying decision, why would you think that they would impact on the buying decision of someone who will buy your home?

Real Estate Agents Don't Sell Homes

Unfortunately, few people realise that 95% of the most important steps in a marketing campaign will have been carried out well before the first open home is even held. Whether these steps have been done well or poorly will have a much greater impact on the success of the campaign than the open home itself. Most people incorrectly think that the open house is a much more important step than it actually is, when in reality the way it is conducted cannot compromise the success of an otherwise strong campaign, or save a poor one.

95% of the most important steps in a marketing campaign will have been carried out well before the first open home is even held

---

As an example, I remember the very first property my wife and I bought to live in. The agent who showed it to us was very poorly presented and wasn't very friendly, helpful or competent. None of this mattered because the property was in the location we were searching, it presented well and was within our budget. We have also attended countless open homes where the real estate agent had a very nice car, wore an expensive suit, had glossy brochures and magazines and was friendly, helpful and very knowledgeable. Again, none of this made any difference, because many of those properties were in a poor condition, poorly presented, overpriced, or a combination of these.

The truth about open homes is that they attract a large number of unqualified people, most of whom will be 'sticky beaks'. They will include your neighbours, people from down the road and others who happen to be in the area at the time. When there are 15 to 20 people coming through your home in a short space of 30 to 40 minutes, it will make it very hard for anybody, including the agent, to pick the truly interested parties from those that are just looking, 'tyre kicking' or 'sticky beaking'.

In this situation, it is much harder to spend valuable time with the serious few whose intention is to purchase, not to mention keeping an eye on everyone to make sure that the 'sticky beaks' don't turn into sticky fingers. Theft is not an uncommon occurrence at busy open homes, especially where there is more than one way in and out of the property. A fake name and telephone number is all too easy to give to an agent for someone with such questionable intentions. Real estate agents will generally deny that this ever happens.

Real Estate Agents Don't Sell Homes

Because of the short duration of open homes, there is often a higher concentration of people in a given space, some of whom may be your potential buyers. Many couples attend open homes and talk to each other about what they see, and because no home can please everyone, they will point out and talk about aspects of your home which they think are negative. No real estate agent can control the negative things people say about your home within earshot of your potential buyers.

No real estate agent can control the negative things people say about your home within earshot of your potential buyers

---

Unfortunately, those truly interested potential buyers may not have noticed those 'negative' aspects of your home if they didn't overhear these conversations. On the flip side of a busy open home is one where there is only one visitor, which does happen sometimes. If this person is truly interested in your home, but sees that they are the only one looking at it, they will factor the lack of interest into their negotiation and may attempt to negotiate the price down or give a very low offer.

Even though open homes may be advertised quite a number of days or even weeks ahead, there will always be people who will not be able to attend that relatively short 30 or 40 minute inspection for whatever reason. They will invariably call the agent shortly after, asking to see the property later that afternoon or in the next day or two.

Many busy agents will decline this request and ask the person to come to the next open, which could be the following weekend – a week away. There is a risk of losing a potential buyer by not making the home available at any other time other than the scheduled opens. As with most opportunities in life, you have to strike while the iron is hot, which in this case means being flexible enough to show the property to potential buyers, especially those who make the effort to call and ask to see it.

Real estate agents argue for open homes by saying that having a crowd of people in the property all at once creates a feeling of competition or scarcity for the property and therefore will entice people to make higher offers sooner. This is not necessarily true.

A great example that comes to mind is that of a good friend of mine who bought his first home from a traditional real estate agent. He and his wife went to one of the open homes and they liked the house. At the open home, they overheard another couple discussing the offer that they would submit to the agent based on an earlier discussion with that agent.

Upon hearing this, my friend thought that they would try their luck by submitting a similar offer that was only $2,000 higher. Their offer was accepted and they bought the house, despite the fact that they would have been willing to pay more. This is just another example and reason why you should never hold an open home when selling your property.

Open homes attract all sorts of people, many of whom have no real interest in the property at all. Potential buyers at an inspection are often very good at reading the vibes of their competition and can pick them from those who are just having a sticky beak. Often, not knowing who their competition is, is a more powerful emotional and psychological influencer for your buyer than seeing them face-to-face. The imagination of people has a tendency to inflate the threat of competition when they don't know who the competition is. In the case of your buyer, of course it helps them if they know who their competition is (better the devil you know). For you, selling your property, it is better the devil the buyer doesn't know.

Inspections by appointment

The best way to achieve this is also the best way to address all the shortcomings of an open home. Of course I am talking about none other than an inspection by appointment. With this method the home is generally shown to one or two parties at a time. After seeing the advertisement online, people will email or telephone to ask to view the home.

People who take the effort to email or telephone to make an appointment are more serious and better qualified prospects.

Ninety-five percent of the marketing will have been done up to this point, and the better it has been executed, the more successful the campaign will be. The people who take the time and effort to email or telephone to make an appointment are usually far more serious and better qualified prospects than most of the people who attend an open home. They qualify themselves by simply making the effort to ask for an appointment, and they wouldn't do that

Real Estate Agents Don't Sell Homes

if they were not seriously interested enough in your home.

When only serious and qualified prospects inspect your property, they are fewer in number, and because they generally see the property one, two or three at a time, it is much easier to deal with them and gauge their level of interest in your home. Inspections by appointment also eliminate the chance of a 'sticky beak' infecting the positive impressions of a potential buyer with their negative comments.

Other advantages of inspections by appointment are the reduced chance of missing out on a potential buyer between open homes and the reduced risk of theft. Prospects who attend an inspection by appointment will often have no idea about the competition they are up against for your property and this can be used to your benefit.

For those who insist on creating a feeling of competition amongst their prospective buyers, an inspection by appointment can be used far more effectively to achieve this than a traditional open home. Most of the enquiries from potential buyers tend to be received within the first two weeks of a home being listed for sale. When an appointment for an inspection is made with a prospective buyer, additional requests to see the property from other buyers can be scheduled for the same time.

This usually results in two, three and even four interested

and qualified parties coming to inspect at the same time. This is far more effective than having ten or fifteen sticky beaks represented by your neighbours, people from down the street and those that happen to be driving by at the time. Competition will always be more intense between serious buyers, even if they are fewer in number than the typical 'tyre kickers' at an open home.

When you go to an open home, you generally expect to see a number of other people looking as well, but imagine if you made an appointment to see a property, expecting to be the only one there and you see one, two or three other people looking as well. You will immediately get the impression that there must be great interest in the property.

There is one twist that significantly increases both the effectiveness and success of an inspection by appointment and therefore the outcome of the campaign. Most people would never think of this twist because of the decades of conditioning to which the Australian public has been subjected to by the traditional real estate sales industry. After most (95%) of the marketing campaign has been completed, whenever possible home owners should always open their home to prospects directly.

There are several benefits to doing this. Firstly, nobody knows your home better than you, which means that nobody is better qualified to point out all the positive aspects of your home, especially those that are not obvious. A good example of this is when a client of ours was showing me through his home and we arrived at the ensuite, which was on the second level. There was a skylight above the shower and the owner explained how at certain times of the day, when you showered, there was a rainbow created by the sun shining through the skylight, so effectively you would be showering under your personal rainbow.

This may seem like an odd example, but there are plenty of positive aspects to many homes, which may not be evident to a buyer at the time of an inspection. These may include the way the sun lights up certain rooms at certain times of the day in winter, creating a pleasant warm atmosphere and a bright airy feel to the room. It could be how the rainbow lorikeets flock to a certain part of the garden to feed at a particular time each day.

By pointing these things out, you are not selling your home. We discussed earlier that a home cannot be sold, no matter who says what, because if the prospect doesn't like it, then no rainbows, sunshine or rainbow lorikeets will make any difference. Pointing these things out simply helps to paint a picture of your property as a home instead of just a house. People prefer to buy homes to houses and they will pay more for a home.

Having said this, you should not feel any obligation to talk to the buyer at all. If you cannot think of any positives to point out, which may not be obvious at the time of the inspection, then simply let the buyer have a look around. This is what they would do anyway at an open home and this is how they will make up their mind about whether to purchase your home or not.

No real estate agent will know as much about your home as you.

Another advantage of showing buyers your home directly is the ability to answer most of their questions that relate to the home. No real estate agent will know as much about your home as you, therefore when they are asked questions by potential buyers they have two options. The first is to remember to ask you and then remember to respond to the buyer, which could take days. The second and easiest option is to just make something up. If you can answer most questions easily, then you will help speed up the buying decision.

In some instances, you may be aware of certain issues or problems with your home that are not obvious or which may only be of concern at certain times, such as long periods of heavy tropical rain. You have to remember that no home is perfect and this is why most buyers will pay for a building and pest report.

If you suspect that an issue may be identified by such a report, then it may be wise to fix it, so that it doesn't turn potential buyers away. Otherwise, you should not feel obligated to point out any issues with your property. If this makes you feel bad for not being truthful, then remember that outsourcing this to an agent won't make you any more truthful – it will, however, be a very expensive exercise in commissions.

One of the biggest advantages of welcoming a buyer to your home is the opportunity to build rapport on a personal level. Previous clients of ours have commented that they believed that they were able to achieve a higher price for their home by developing a reasonable relationship with the buyer. Of course this won't always happen and it doesn't need to, but getting to know the buyer even a little bit often helps in making the final stretch of the sale that much smoother.

The initial reaction of some people to showing a buyer their home might be: "I'm not confident or qualified to do this" or "I can't be bothered with this inconvenience".

In answer to the first reaction, you need neither confidence nor competence to do this, as neither has an impact on the success of an inspection. Remember: 95% of the marketing that matters, has already happened before any inspection. People come to an inspection to look at the property and don't care about who opens the door for them. This is why many real estate agencies and busy agents send their juniors to hold open homes and this is why people still buy properties from agents who are poorly presented, unhelpful, unfriendly, inexperienced and even incompetent.

With regards to bothering with the 'inconvenience' of showing one or three potential buyers your home at a time that suits you, I would argue that having to pack up and leave your home for an hour, while groups of 10–20 people – most of whom are sticky beaks – stampede through your home, is far less convenient. Not only is it an illusion to think that it is more convenient to outsource this task to a real estate agent, it is also the most expensive illusion at 2.5% of the sale price of your home plus GST on average.

There are some important things in life that cannot or should not be outsourced, such as taking your spouse out for a date or raising your children. Opening the door to your most valuable asset – your home – should also be in this same category. There is simply too much at stake for you to outsource this to someone else.

Notes

Myth 5:
"I am an expert negotiator, trained to get you a higher price"

Portraying themselves as professional negotiators is another sales tactic that agents use to impress you and win your business. They want to convince you that they are the only people who can negotiate a higher price for you and a price which would justify their commission.

Most people are surprised to find out that the very short course that real estate agents must complete in order to become licensed involves no detailed training on negotiation techniques. In other words, they may be no more of an expert at negotiation than anybody else.

The other problem with using a traditional real estate agent is that vendors already start with a significant disadvantage of having to pay a commission. If a property is valued at $600,000, a real estate agent needs to achieve a sale price of $616,500 just to cover their 2.5% commission plus GST. Buyers are unlikely to pay $16,500 more for a property just so that you can pay for your real estate agent.

How much you can walk away with after their expenses, should be a much more important figure.

To truly justify using a real estate agent, you would need to achieve an even higher sale price, otherwise you are only employing them to cover their cost. Traditional real estate agents will always talk about how much they can sell your property for, but not about how much you can walk away with after their expenses, which should be a much more important figure for you than what you sell for.

Often agents will boast about how much above the asking price they have sold properties for. This automatically implies that they are fantastic negotiators and this is exactly what we are supposed to believe. In actual fact, the true story is a little different. I have encountered a number of cases where real estate agents listed properties considerably below their market value using a tactic called 'bait' pricing.

This tactic involves setting a lower price than what the home is really worth in the hope of generating lots of interest in the property and starting a bidding war among prospective buyers. Negotiating a 'higher' price is easy when a home is advertised below its market value. Many agents will brag about the higher price they negotiated, when in fact they simply achieved the actual market value, after starting with an unrealistically low listing price.

Bait pricing is illegal, and is an offence under the Australian Consumer Law. If, despite being illegal, bait pricing was not practised widely enough, you would have to wonder why there were recent amendments to the Property Stock and Business Agents Act of 2002 in New South Wales that came into effect in January 2016. These amendments specifically target underquoting by real estate agents.

An agent will only lose $250 in commissions, by convincing you that you should sell for $10,000 less.

The truth is that real estate agents have very little incentive to negotiate a higher price for your property. For them to work hard to negotiate an extra $10,000 for you, their potential reward is only $250 in additional commission –

not enough money for them to delay sealing the deal to get paid. On the flipside, an agent will only lose $250 in commissions, by convincing you that you should sell for $10,000 less than what you could possibly receive. This is why real estate commissions are a terrible way to remunerate someone to help you sell your home. Instead of serving as an incentive to achieve a higher sale price, more often than not, it does the exact opposite.

Most people also don't know that if another agent finds a buyer for your home, your agent will have to share their commission with that agent. The other agent could be somebody from the same office, a competing agency, or it could even be a buyer's agent.

Just imagine a scenario where the agent you are using has found a buyer who is willing to pay a maximum of $500,000 for your property and, without you knowing, another agent introduces another potential buyer to your agent. This buyer is willing to pay no more than $510,000. The difference between these two buyers is that the second buyer is willing to pay you $10,000 more. However, selling to this buyer would mean that your agent would receive $6,125 less, after sharing half of the 2.5% commission with the introducing agent.

This is an astounding conflict of interest! Imagine the pressure on your agent to either present you the offer for

$500,000, on which they would earn a $12,500 commission, or the offer for $510,000 and receiving only a $6,375 share of the full commission. Most real estate agents don't want to risk losing half of their commission to another agent and, as a result, they will likely pressure you to sign a contract as soon as possible with a buyer they find. This is another disincentive for them to prolong the sale process by getting involved in negotiations.

Most real estate agents know that they will not successfully sell every house they list for various reasons. One of these reasons is the unrealistic price expectation of some stubborn vendors. As a result, agents play a numbers game where for instance out of every 500 letterbox drops, they will list six properties and end up selling four. Despite the work, time, effort and cost that goes into the letter box drops and marketing the listings, they will only get paid for the properties they sell, irrelevant of what price they fetch.

A sale at almost any price is the only real measure of success for an agent.

In other words, securing a sale at almost any price is the only real measure of success for an agent, not the sale price they achieve. As I mentioned earlier, a higher sale price does not make much difference to their commission, but the quicker they can sell your home, the quicker they can move onto the next one to keep the numbers game up. **The simple fact that they operate in a system where a sale is more important than the sale price, compromises their incentive to negotiate for you.**

Negotiation is one of the most highly misunderstood steps in the process of marketing and selling a home. Many real estate agents make negotiation out to be a difficult, thrashed out, UN peacekeeping or hostage negotiation style process, when nothing could be further from the truth. If the marketing has been done correctly, often there is very little, if any, need at all to negotiate.

You may simply be able to choose from a number of offers and select the one that has the highest price and the best conditions. Protracted negotiations usually occur if the property was incorrectly advertised at a 'bait' price below market value, as I outlined earlier, or at a higher price than what it is actually worth. If a property that has been advertised at above its market value does generate interest, it will only be from potential buyers at a lower, realistic price point, which will start the negotiation process. If the property is priced and marketed correctly, then there is often no need to negotiate at all.

Our marketing efforts for a recent client resulted in four qualified and strong offers being received within the first two weeks. The highest of these had a price that was above the initial expectation of our client, with only the standard 14 day building and pest condition and the 21 day finance condition. Considering that this offer was above our client's expectation, and they were very happy with it, they chose not to negotiate at all. This is the kind of result we would expect after a well conducted campaign in a standard metropolitan suburb.

More often than not, if any negotiation does take place, it doesn't even happen verbally, but rather by email. In Queensland, offers can be submitted on a standard REIQ (Real Estate Institute of Queensland) contract, and this is what we insist on. With such offers, the vendor has the option of either countersigning that offer or simply crossing out the dollar figure, writing their own higher dollar figure, initialling it and then sending it back to the buyer. The buyer then has the option of either countersigning and accepting that offer or crossing it out, initialling it and returning it. If this occurs, it doesn't normally happen any more than once or twice in a transaction.

In cases where the marketing campaign was well conducted and negotiation still takes place, the impact that negotiations have on the final price is much smaller than the difference made by the campaign itself and the three important steps of the marketing process of Presentation, Pricing and Promotion.

By way of another example, a previous client of ours was expecting to sell his townhouse for $650,000. With the help of our strategic marketing campaign, he received a very strong and clean offer for $690,000, which was the record price in the area at the time. Our client became emboldened by this offer and thought that he could extract a higher price still by negotiating. He was successful, but only to the tune of $5,000. Many might rightly say that that is a lot of money and it is better in their pocket than the buyer's, and they may be right.

The point is that this $5,000 was not as significant as the extra $40,000 that the campaign generated in comparison to the vendor's expectations. When a well conducted campaign can make such a big difference to the final price and well exceed expectations, it is often better not to squeeze every last drop from a buyer so that both parties can feel good about having achieved a win/win transaction. This can help keep a good relationship going all the way up to settlement, ensuring that everything progresses smoothly.

It is strange that when buying a home many people are completely comfortable in negotiating with an agent, yet when it comes to selling that same home, they feel like they need an 'expert' negotiator to do it on their behalf.

It is strange that when buying a home many people are completely comfortable in negotiating with an agent, yet when it comes to selling that same home, they feel like they need an 'expert' negotiator to do it on their behalf.

Many people do feel uncomfortable with the thought of negotiation and are completely repulsed by it. However, when some people think of negotiating, they think of a high pressure, adversarial situation, where one party can only win if the other loses. This is completely the wrong way to think about the process, but another book would need to be dedicated to explaining why this is the case and how successful negotiations should be conducted. It is enough to say here that if negotiations do take place, the process we advocate is neither high pressure, nor adversarial.

Real Estate Agents Don't Sell Homes

We normally insist that all offers are submitted in writing (on a contract in Queensland), with sufficient time for the vendor to consider which one to accept. An offer in writing – especially on a contract – confirms that the buyer is serious. If negotiating is required, depending on the client, we often advise for it to occur in writing – mostly email – in order to make the process less personal and emotional. This helps many people overcome their unfounded fear of the process. After each response or counter offer is received, we encourage the vendor to thank the buyer for the offer and let them know that they will respond within 24 hours. This provides sufficient time for us to consult with the vendor and formulate a tactical and well considered response.

In effect, the process we help our clients with redefines the meaning of negotiation and turns it into a series of offers and counter-offers that occur in writing, with sufficient time between them to plan a strategic response. Vendors can benefit greatly from understanding that negotiation is not what real estate agents make it out to be, it doesn't necessarily form part of every sale, and agents are neither experts in the process, nor incentivised sufficiently to do it well on your behalf.

Notes

Myth 6:
The local area expert

Many real estate agents advertise themselves proudly as the local area experts, which again sounds very impressive, but most people don't think about what this really means and whether it has any significance. Real estate agents become local area experts because they are forced to. When they have to conduct between three to five open homes every weekend, it becomes nearly impossible to cover distances of up to 30, 40 or 50 kilometres between each home. They are constrained by the fact that they insist on holding the open homes themselves.

In other words, they are forced to concentrate on their local geographic area, because the way the industry works leaves them no choice. Naturally, they have tried to turn this negative into a positive by pitching themselves as the local experts in their area. So, if you see an agent active in your area, it doesn't necessarily mean that they are experts or even any good, but simply that they have a narrower focus on a well-defined territory. Many people choose to use an agent based on seeing their sold signs in the neighbourhood, without asking the owners of these homes if they were happy with the agent or the price they received.

Knowing values has nothing to do with achieving the highest sale price.

A real estate agent who claims to be a local area expert will say that they know the prices better than anybody else. This is probably true, but it does not mean that they will achieve the highest price for you, because knowing values has nothing to do with achieving the highest sale price. Besides, getting the price right is only one of the three elements of a successful marketing campaign, next to Presentation and Promotion.

Knowing the local prices well also won't stop many agents from quoting you an inflated sale price in order to win your listing. Knowing a suburb and its prices intimately is helpful, but is not the most important component of a successful marketing campaign and achieving the highest price.

As an example, we recently assisted a client in the sale of

their home in a suburb we did not know much about. Even though it was a suburb of the same city of Brisbane where we live, it may as well have been a suburb of Melbourne or Sydney as far as we were concerned. After about 2-3 hours of thorough research of the suburb, we knew enough about it to be able to narrow down the price range to within an acceptably tight band.

Using a variety of online tools, we can find out enough about any suburb in Australia to enable a successful marketing campaign that achieves the highest possible price for a home. Some of these tools are free, like Realestate.com.au, while others require a subscription, such as RPData or Price Finder. (Similar sites exist in other countries across the world.)

Once we knew the price band in which we could expect offers to be received, it was a matter of conducting the important elements of the marketing mix, which make up 95% of the entire campaign. Part of this was how to strategically communicate the price zone, which is far more important than knowing exactly what the property will sell for.

Together with the other parts of the marketing campaign, communicating the price zone in a tactical way generated strong, qualified interest in the property, without either misguiding potential buyers or putting a cap on what an emotional buyer would pay. It turned out that the property sold for a record price for its category in the area, which was more than what both the owner and I were expecting it to fetch.

Another example was our very first interstate client who was selling her home in a suburb of Adelaide. Before we were engaged to assist with the marketing, we had no idea that this suburb had even existed. Of course this was totally irrelevant, because after 2-3 hours of thorough research we were able to establish a reasonably tight price band within which the property was expected to sell. Thanks to our negotiation strategies and techniques, we were able to help this client achieve a sale price that was towards the top of this price band while saving them over $12,000 in real estate agent commissions and marketing fees – and all this from two thousand kilometres away.

It is of little value to know exactly what a property will sell for and, as mentioned earlier in this book, it is also almost impossible. Being a local area expert unfortunately does not guarantee that a real estate agent will be any better at effectively selling your home and putting more money in your pocket.

Notes

Myth 7:
The frenzy of an auction achieves a higher price

Most people don't know that auctions are generally better for the agent and also the buyer, than they are for the seller. One of the reasons an agent would recommend an auction is that it is another 'service' from which they make a considerable amount of money, partly due to the intensive campaign that they recommend to accompany it.

The other reason many real estate agents prefer auctions is that it has a relatively short campaign period and a fixed end date with no conditions, which means that they are likely to receive their commission sooner. Even if the property is passed in at auction, they will generally use the outcome to pressure the vendor to 'meet the market' and make a deal with the highest bidder.

Most sellers who agree to auction their property don't realise that on auction day, the pressure on them can be just as great as the pressure on the buyers, sometimes even more so. If the bidding doesn't reach the vendor's expected price, real estate agents will coerce the seller on the day by saying the market is here and it has spoken and this is what you have to sell for if you want to sell. What they won't mention is that auctions turn many people off due to the pressured environment.

Many of your potential buyers will stay away while the people that are there will not be a true reflection of the 'market', because many people hate auctions more than they like the property being auctioned. It is easy to mistake the crowd at an auction for a 'big turnout of the market', when in fact the circus of the event will naturally attract a mostly unqualified crowd of onlookers.

As an example of the pressure at an auction, my wife and I attended one in a more established and expensive suburb of Brisbane. The property market was quite buoyant at the time and the large turnout reflected this. The home was being sold by an elderly couple, who were in the front yard within view of the crowd.

As the bidding started, it became apparent that there were only two serious contenders, despite the considerable swarm of people and the intensive and expensive campaign that led to that moment. In addition to the auctioneer, two agents were 'working' the crowd, focusing mainly on the two serious bidders. When the bidding stalled prior to reaching the reserve price, we watched as the two agents and the auctioneer all towered over this elderly couple in a way that would have made me feel extremely intimidated. I can only imagine the pressure this elderly couple was under, which was further compounded by the throng of onlookers.

The most obvious observation most of us would have about an auction is that the price goes up, which is a good thing, so auctions must be good, and this is exactly what many agents want us to think. There are many less obvious factors that work against the seller and therefore benefit the buyer.

All that buyers have to do is outbid their competition by one extra bid, which could be as low as $1,000.

One of these is the reserve price, which is the lowest price that the seller wants to achieve. Once the bidding reaches this price, the auctioneer has to disclose it by saying that the property is 'on the market'. This has the effect of showing the vendor's cards by revealing their lowest acceptable price to all the bidders at the auction. This is very one-sided as the bidders don't have to reveal the highest price they are willing to pay. All that buyers have to do is outbid their competition by one extra bid, which could be as low as $1,000.

Consider the example of a property which is valued at approximately $600,000. There are three very interested people who want to buy this property but they all have three very different budgets. The first person may have a budget of $550,000, the second may have a budget of $570,000 and the third may have a budget of $620,000.

On auction day, when the price reaches and exceeds $550,000 the first buyer will drop out, when it passes $570,000 the second buyer will also drop out and the third bidder may only need to offer $5,000 more than the second highest bidder's budget to buy the property for $575,000. This is despite the fact that the bidder would have been prepared to pay $620,000 and may even have been approved for this amount by their bank.

In other words, the buyer saved $45,000 and the seller received $45,000 less than they could have otherwise. It goes without saying that the vendor would still have had to pay at least a hefty commission at around 2.5% + GST, or just under $16,000 – not counting the thousands in marketing costs – to their agent for the 'privilege' of losing out on $45,000. This is exactly why many savvy buyers prefer to buy at auction, where they can often get a very nice discount.

The inherent disadvantage of an auction is that most of the cards are on the table for all to see. All bidders know the vendor's lowest price, once the reserve has been reached, and each bidder knows what the last bid was. The only unknown is the highest price that the strongest bidder is willing to pay. At an auction, this will never be known as the winning bidder doesn't have to pay their highest price, only a little more than the budget of the second highest bidder.

People thinking of selling their home need to understand that auctions are an expensive, stressful and ineffective way to go about this. The process favours the agent and the buyer and so the outcome for the seller is compromised. One example of a much better method of extracting the highest price from potential buyers is by letting all buyers know that offers will be collected over a short, specified period – of a week or two – and that they have one chance to submit their best bid. It needs to be clarified at the outset that the price they offer needs to be such that they are willing to walk away from the property if theirs is not the best. This method has a far better chance of flushing out the highest possible bid for a property than an auction does, provided that the marketing campaign was executed well.

Notes

The better way to sell – trust the process, not an agent

The topics covered in this book are by no means an exhaustive debunking of the real estate sales industry, but by highlighting the main seven myths that have become deeply ingrained in the Australian psyche, you will no doubt question what you think you know and to look for an alternative.

To save Australians from making one of the most expensive mistakes of their lives – selling with a real estate agent.

Knowing what I know about this industry, I promised myself never to let any of my family or friends become victims of it when it comes time for them to sell a property.

If my family and friends are worthy of my help, then so are all my fellow Australians. After I came to this conclusion, I made it my mission to save Australians from making one of the most expensive mistakes of their lives – selling with a real estate agent.

I quickly realised that I had to also warn people of making the second most expensive mistake, which is to sell privately. People who attempt to do this without knowing and following the recipe risk leaving lots of money on the table.

There is a process or recipe that sells a property and this recipe doesn't care who follows it.

As I mentioned at the beginning of this book, there is a process or recipe that sells a property and this recipe doesn't care who follows it. This means that it doesn't have to be a real estate agent. You certainly don't have to pay anywhere near 2.5% plus GST in commissions, in addition to unnecessarily high marketing fees – which can be up to 1% of the value of the property – in order to have this recipe working for you. The recipe itself consists of three parts – Presentation, Pricing and Promotion – which when executed well, make all the difference to the success of any property marketing campaign.

Presentation

Of the three parts, Presentation is the trickiest, because it encompasses so many factors. Think back to the time when you were looking for a home to buy and you were comparing different properties with various qualities of presentation. All other things being equal, you were probably drawn to those that were inviting and homely, in addition to being light, fresh, relatively spacious and modern in appearance. These are the hallmarks of a well presented home, which most people look for, especially if they will be living in it.

Buyers are willing to pay more for a lifestyle than they are for bricks and mortar.

Not only do well presented homes sell quicker, they also fetch a higher price, and there are two reasons for this. Firstly, people see that they don't have to spend time, money and effort to bring the home up to their standard and secondly, because the presentation itself appeals to their emotions. This second reason is the most important reason to focus on presentation, because buyers are willing to pay more for a lifestyle than they are for bricks and mortar.

You don't necessarily have to spend huge amounts of money to improve the presentation and often the most cost effective solutions can have the biggest impact. There are many ways to improve the presentation of your home, with some of the most obvious ones being repairs and renovations, gardening, cleaning, painting, de-cluttering and styling or staging.

It is not always necessary to have an exceptional standard of presentation, as long as it is better than most of your competition, because when you put your home on the market, it may need to compete for buyers alongside other similar homes. If your presentation is below par and there is not much to make your home stand out from the competition, buyers will focus on the price as the only remaining point of differentiation. This is why people who market a poorly presented home are likelier to have to accept a lower price.

The importance of an excellent photographer cannot be overemphasized when it comes to presentation. The best presentation can be compromised by an average photographer, because the pictures are what people see first when browsing on real estate websites. If the photos are not enticing enough, many people may not even bother to take the time for an inspection. For a relatively modest investment of between $150 and $300, the right photographer can make a significant difference.

Pricing

Pricing a home for sale is a tactical play that is also crucially important. It is not enough to know how much the home is 'worth' or what price range it is expected to sell within. The price has to be communicated so that it entices as many qualified people as possible in the target price range to an inspection. The price has to be pitched in a way that is not misleading or too specific, making it hard for an emotional buyer to pay more if they fall in love with the home.

This is why I recommend against putting an exact dollar value on a property, because if the buyer sees $545,000 as the advertised price, it will be hard to extract much more than this from even someone who feels like they've found their dream home. Price is one of the most important criteria buyers use to sort through the number of properties available for sale, so they do expect to see at least a rough guide, and many people will be frustrated and even angry when they come across a property that is advertised with the words 'make an offer' or 'by negotiation'.

Many vendors incorrectly think that if they start with a higher price, they will have room to negotiate down, but the problem with this method is that it will often scare off many potential buyers who think that the property is too expensive and that you are not flexible in your price. It can also scare off those people who do not like to get involved in protracted negotiations when buying.

The last thing you should do is to turn away a segment of your potential buyers even before they've had a chance to see and fall in love with your property. This is exactly what happens when vendors want to 'test' the market, by starting with an unrealistically high price. Buyers aren't silly and they know that a seller who is testing the market is greedy and not serious about selling. Home buyers can spot these properties from a mile away because they often sit on the market for months or even years. The market will start to think that there is something wrong with the property for not having sold sooner and this is not the kind of 'bad smell' that a serious vendor wants their property to have.

You should also establish your 'walk away' price, which is the price below which you will not negotiate under or sell for. It is important to be realistic when setting this value, however, thorough market research will help with this.

Many sale campaigns fail due to unrealistic expectations on the part of home sellers.

In summary, there are three aspects to pricing: Establishing the price range or band, strategically pitching this range to the market, and knowing your 'walk away' price.

Promotion

The last of the three parts in the marketing process, but by no means the least important, is Promotion. When selling a home, you want the greatest amount of exposure to the right target market. Thankfully this is much easier these days than it was before the days of the internet.

Estimates and statistics vary slightly, but the percentage of Australians who find a property to buy on the two main real estate listing websites (Realestate.com.au and Domain) is above 94% and growing. These are by far the best channels to target your buyers. It is also relatively cost effective to have access to both of these portals for approximately $600 until the property is sold. You no longer need to use a traditional real estate agent to do this. Again, similar sites exist in other countries across the world.

Most real estate agents will continue to push advertising in newspapers and, even though these may increase your audience somewhat, it is simply not cost effective or necessary for a great result, especially when most printed newspapers have a falling readership. Most people are aware of the 80/20 principle, otherwise known as the Pareto Principle, where 80% of your results come from 20% of your efforts. You can achieve an even better ratio than this when promoting your property, because you can reach about 94% of your potential buyers for 10% of the marketing budget, which many real estate agents propose, and which can amount to 1% of the value of your home.

It is neither realistic, nor cost effective to have exposure to 100% of your target market and it is very easy to fall into the trap of spending many thousands of dollars in a futile effort to try.

If the cost to have access to about 94% of your target market is $600, then the cost of accessing every extra percentage of your target market will have an exponentially higher cost and a diminishing rate of return. It is very easy to spend thousands of dollars for a relatively small number of additional prospects. It can very quickly become a wasteful way to spend your money.

In addition to the above mentioned three P's, there is a fourth one that is often overlooked, which is Preparation. In order to achieve the best results with optimally presenting a home for sale, you cannot start preparing early enough. The sooner you know what clever, cosmetic and strategic changes are best to carry out on your home, the sooner you can start budgeting and planning for it.

Most of the necessary work can be carried out by handymen at a surprisingly low cost, however, the better ones can be booked out for weeks or even months in advance. One week before looking to put your home on the market is not the time to start thinking about what cosmetic alterations should be carried out by who and when.

To achieve the best results with optimally presenting a home for sale, you cannot start preparing early enough.

Marketing as an investment

There are obviously several expenses associated with selling your home. Instead of viewing them as expenses, it will serve you better to consider them as investments. Just like making any other investment, you want to achieve the highest return. Most people will have a limited budget for marketing, which makes it very important to allocate it in a way that will help to achieve the highest sale price, but even more importantly, the highest possible balance in your bank account after all expenses are paid.

Consider a scenario where you would like to sell your home, which in its current, slightly tired condition, is valued at exactly $600,000 by a registered valuer. You decide that you do not want to spend any more than $16,000 in marketing the home. If you were to list the home in its current state with a real estate agent, they would charge you over $16,000 in commission alone (2.5%+GST) without any advertising fees. This would mean that you would walk away with approximately $584,000 from the sale of your home (for the sake of this illustration I will ignore legal fees, taxes and advertising).

Clever renovations can add three dollars of value for every dollar spent.

Now imagine that, instead of spending it on commissions, you used the same $16,000 to carry out strategic, cosmetic renovations and styling to improve the presentation of your home. We know from experience that well thought out, clever renovations can add three dollars of value for every dollar spent, and often more. In this scenario a three to one return on investment of $16,000 in renovations would increase the value of your home to $648,000. After deducting the renovation expenses you would be left with $632,000 after selling the home.

The difference between pocketing $584,000 and $632,000 is $48,000. Of course the second scenario did not factor in marketing costs. We also know from experience that for around $6,000 to $7,000, it is possible to achieve a highly effective marketing campaign, because we have been doing this for ourselves, our family and our clients for long enough. The campaign I'm referring to does not lack any of the qualities or expertise of the very best real estate agents. As a matter of fact, it often results in a higher sale price.

For the sake of this comparison, let's assume that the total marketing budget was exactly $8,000. The difference in outcome between the two scenarios becomes $40,000. What would you do with an extra $40,000? This is the kind of result that is often achieved simply by better allocating your marketing budget to those costs that have a much higher return on investment. Unfortunately, real estate agent commissions are not one of these expenses.

Some might say that a real estate agent could help to achieve a higher sale price than $600,000 with their negotiation skills and this may be true. However, real estate agents aren't the only people who have negotiation skills and as I mentioned earlier, negotiation is not actually taught to agents in the course they undertake to become registered. Even the very best negotiator has their limits, because there is only so much that anybody is willing to pay for any home when there are other similar properties on offer within a well-defined price range.

Real estate agents aren't the only people who have negotiation skills.

I deliberately started this scenario by mentioning that the home in question was valued by a registered valuer. Assuming that similar homes (before the renovation) are selling at around $600,000, a real estate agent would have had to achieve around $642,000 for the unrenovated home to leave you with the same end result as you would have achieved by renovating. Would you pay more for a tired property sold by a smooth talking agent or for one that was updated, modernised and in great condition?

A better way to sell

If real estate agents don't sell properties; don't make the

process of selling convenient; don't provide value with their 'database' of buyers, the open homes they hold or their local expertise; are neither the expert negotiators they would like us to think, nor incentivised enough to be so, then why should we continue to pay them? The simple answer is that in most cases, we shouldn't!

Only a very small percentage of Australians are truly aware of how the real estate industry really operates and why even the very best real estate agent will always deliver a compromised and poor result, if for no other reason than the excessive commission and marketing fees they charge. You won't find the real estate sales industry telling you the truth that the system is broken and should be reinvented. The existing system suits them just fine and they are happy with the money they are making.

If we always do what we've always done, we'll always get what we always got.

As with anything in life, if we want to achieve better results, we need to do things in a different way, because if we always do what we've always done, we'll always get what we always got. However, we won't have a reason to change the way we do things until we realise that the way we have done them is just not good enough and that there is a much better way. The reason I wrote this book is to help people realise exactly this.

> *Using a traditional real estate agent can never achieve the best result.*

I know for a fact that using a traditional real estate agent can never achieve the best result possible when selling a home. **By this I mean that you will always walk away with significantly less money than you otherwise could, to the tune of $10,000 to $50,000 and even more.**

By thinking that there is nothing wrong with continuing to use traditional real estate agents, because generations before us have done the same, we risk adopting a conformist, herd mentality.

Having said this, it is very useful to have an experienced professional in your corner to guide you through this process, someone who is skilled at applying the steps in the recipe to achieve the best possible result and for the lowest possible expense.

The Stone Age didn't end because we ran out of stone, but because we discovered bronze. Since then, we have moved on from many things, horse drawn carts, typewriters and fax machines and these will soon be joined by the traditional real estate agent. Just like there will always be people who will only stop using typewriters once they stop manufacturing them, there will also be people who will only stop using real estate agents once they cease to exist in the capacity we know them today.

The sooner people adopt better ways of doing things, the sooner they can start to benefit. Conventional methods achieve conventional results and therefore if we want to achieve extraordinary results, we need to consider unconventional methods – or at least methods that initially seem unconventional.

Until recently, the only alternative to a traditional real estate agent was a private sale. There are now many companies offering to help you do this. However, the main benefit from these companies is the ability to advertise on major real estate listing sites (such as Realestate.com.au and Domain in Australia), which addresses only a small portion of one of the three parts of the recipe – Promotion. Due to the lack of personalized service from most of these companies, there is little help with the other two parts of the recipe – Presentation and Pricing – and other assistance, for example with strategies to respond to offers to achieve the highest possible sale price.

Through our business – Revolutionary Real Estate – my wife, Zsofi, and I are among the first of an exciting new group of service providers who are committed to changing the real estate sales industry in Australia. Armed with our knowledge and insight, we have vowed to reinvent the way properties are sold in Australia and revolutionise this industry for the benefit of all home vendors. We know that in the next five to ten years, using a traditional real estate agent to sell your home will be likened by most people to using a typewriter to type a letter today.

Most people need and appreciate help, guidance, coaching, assistance and consulting from an expert.

The disruption that we are introducing to the real estate industry is through a system called the 'assisted private sale'. It recognises that most people need and appreciate help, guidance, coaching, assistance and consulting from an expert, in a way that addresses all the shortcomings of the traditional real estate agent method of selling, at a significantly lower cost. The combination of usually achieving a higher sale price at a significantly lower cost can be life-changing for most people who take advantage of this method.

As marketing strategists and sellers' advocates, our goal is to ensure that home sellers not only maximize the sale price of their home, but also the amount of money they keep from the transaction. I mentioned earlier in this book that 95% of the marketing efforts are done before the first buyer ever inspects your home. This is the most important part of the campaign covering all three parts of the recipe to selling successfully – Presentation, Pricing and Promotion. For this reason, this is the part where we add the greatest value with our efforts and knowledge that stems from our experience with the process.

We know that this process tends to be very highly charged with emotion.

In addition to this, there are three other significant areas where our assistance is invaluable. Firstly, after the successful implementation of the marketing campaign and the three P's, we help our clients with strategies to make it as easy as possible for their buyers to buy. As I mentioned earlier, homes are not sold, they are bought and the less obstacles there are in the way of a buyer to buy, the quicker and smoother the process is.

Secondly, we know that this process tends to be very highly charged with emotion from both the vendor's and the buyer's perspective and can be a real roller coaster ride. Emotions are a distinct liability when it comes to this type of transaction, but they are hard to avoid. The party who is better at managing their emotions is at an advantage and usually benefits more from the transaction. We know what emotions both parties experience in these cases and help our clients – the vendor – to manage their emotions by managing their expectations. At the same time, we help our clients with strategies to appeal to the emotions of the buyer to help them happily pay the highest possible price.

Thirdly, and somewhat built on the second point, we help our clients with negotiation strategies that achieve the highest possible sale price while minimising their emotional investment and risk of losing a potential buyer. We recommend ethical strategies that have been proven to work time and time again, because they play on the same human emotions that most people experience when buying a property.

We find that our process achieves the best results when there is some involvement from the home owner. As I mentioned earlier, the inspections by appointment are one of the easiest steps in the campaign that anybody can do and we encourage the vendor to be involved in this for the reasons I outlined under Myth 4. We consult with all our clients and provide help and assistance all the way up to the point of settlement. The involvement from home owners is no more inconvenient than selling in the traditional way, but the financial benefit from not having to pay a commission and exorbitant marketing fees, while still achieving the highest possible sale price, can well exceed $50,000.

So confident am I that you will see the sense in abandoning the traditional method of selling your home that I will give you a free one-on-one consultation if you mention to me that you have read this book.

Help somebody else join the real estate revolution and pocket tens of thousands of dollars by passing this book on to them.

David Kaity
Revolutionary Real Estate
www.revolutionaryrealestate.com.au

Notes

Notes

Notes

www.ingramcontent.com/pod-product-compliance
Lightning Source LLC
LaVergne TN
LVHW012121070526
838202LV00056B/5824